BIRDWATCHER OR BIRDER

Birdwatching is a popular hobby. Someone who does this is called a birdwatcher or birder. Both birdwatchers and birders are usually amateurs. The scientific study of birds is called ornithology. People who study birds as a profession are called ornithologists.

You don't need to be a avid birder to notice that birds make a wide variety of sounds. With your ears turned on, you could hear all those birds chirping, buzzing, trilling and even singing.If you are not engaging your auditory sense, you may be missing more than half the birds around you in a woodland setting.

You also need to be organised which means you have to keep track of what you have seen and how you identify birds. This birdwatcher's logbook can help you identify certain birds by look and calls, Also, great tools for beginners to help record the birds you have seen.

A Birder's perception of life is different than others, It's their willingness to stand quietly and see what comes.

This book
belongs to.....

Happy Coloring

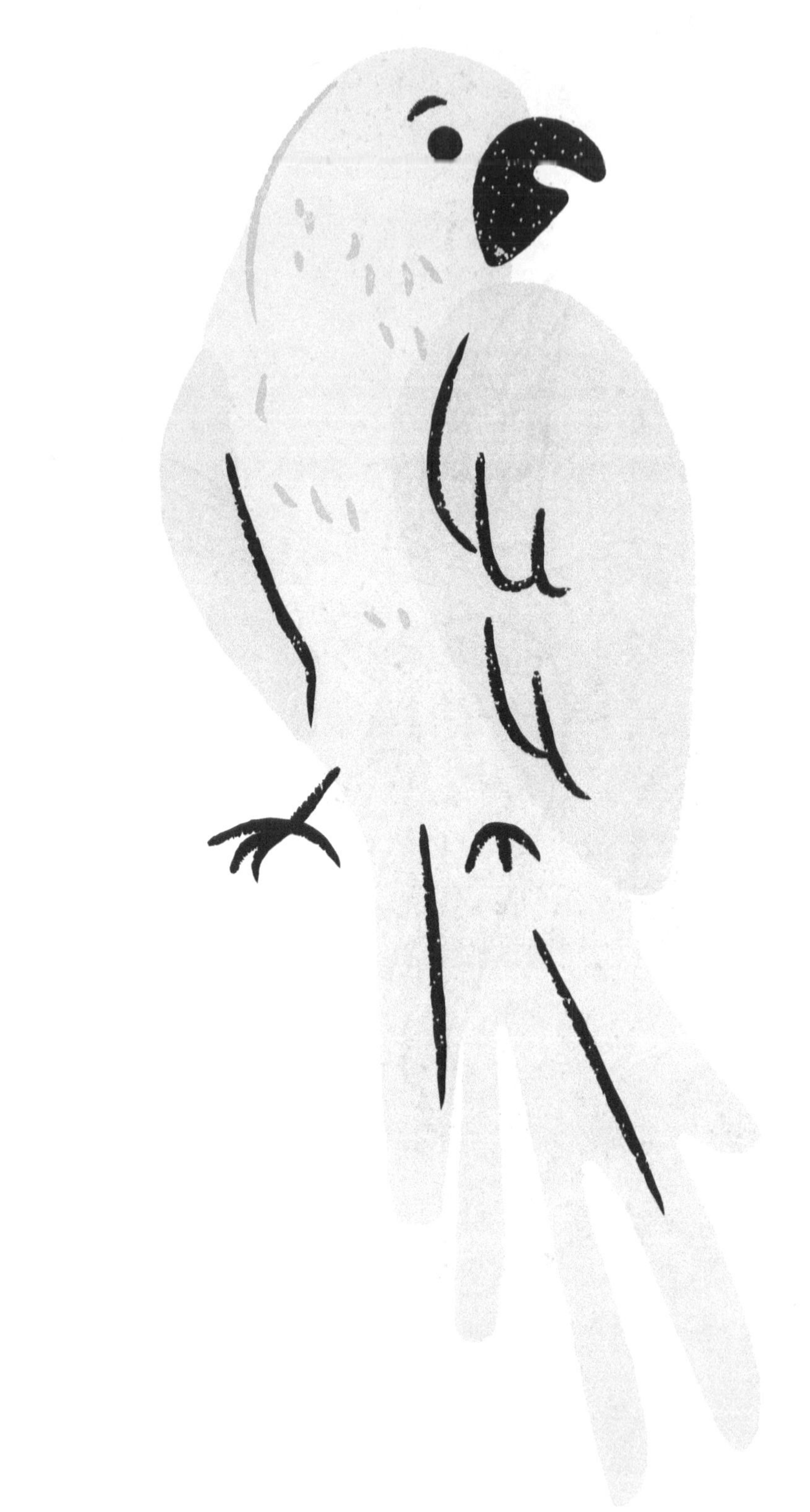

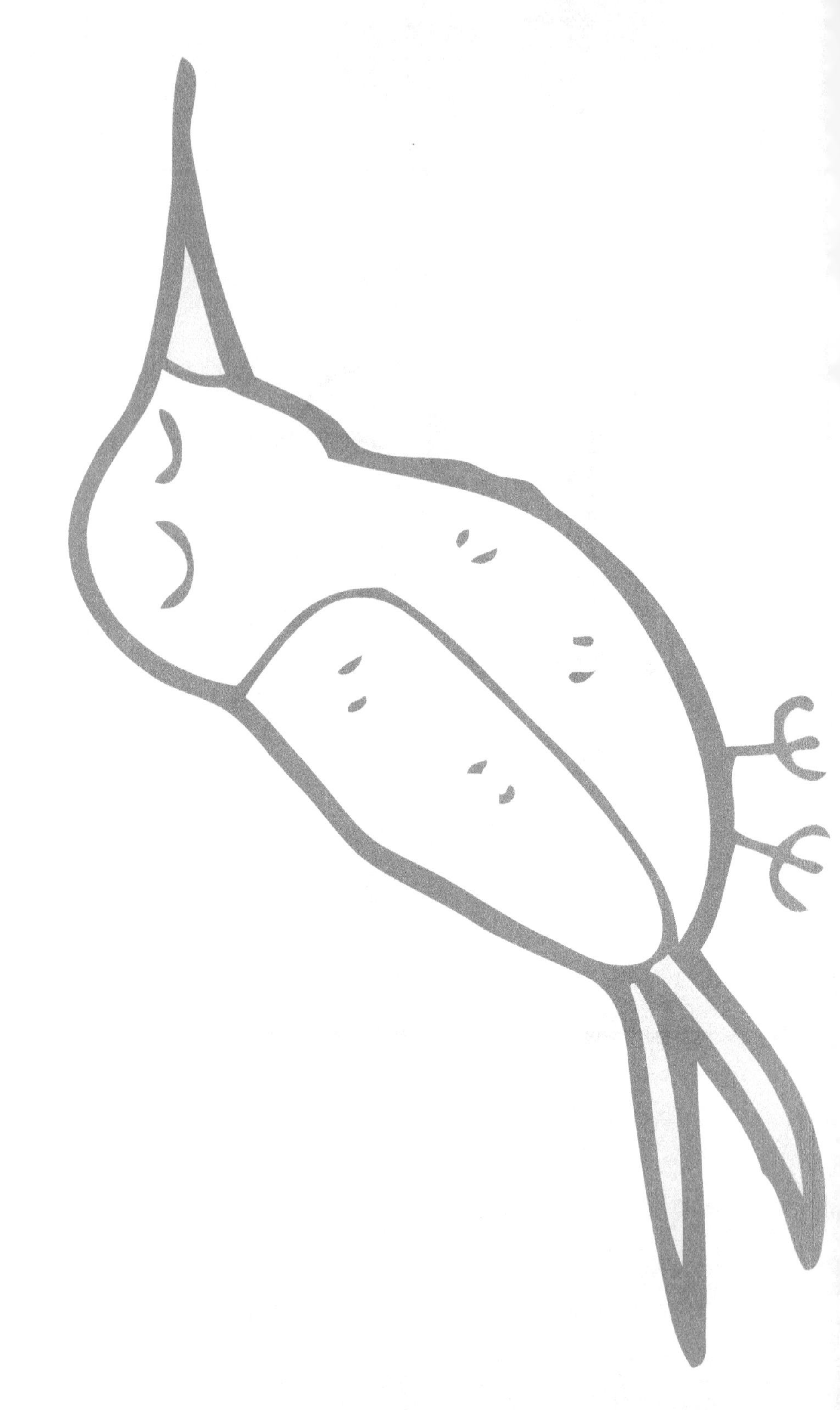

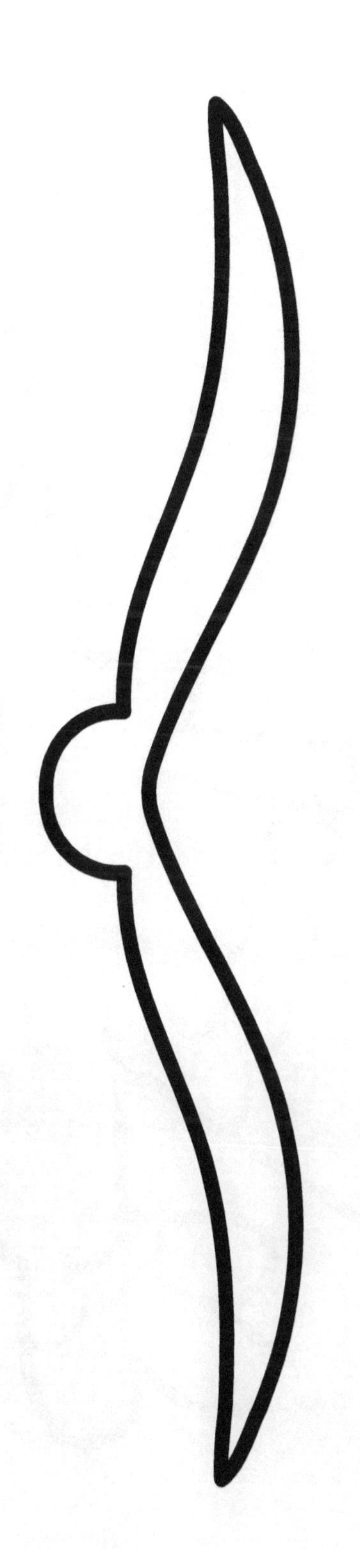

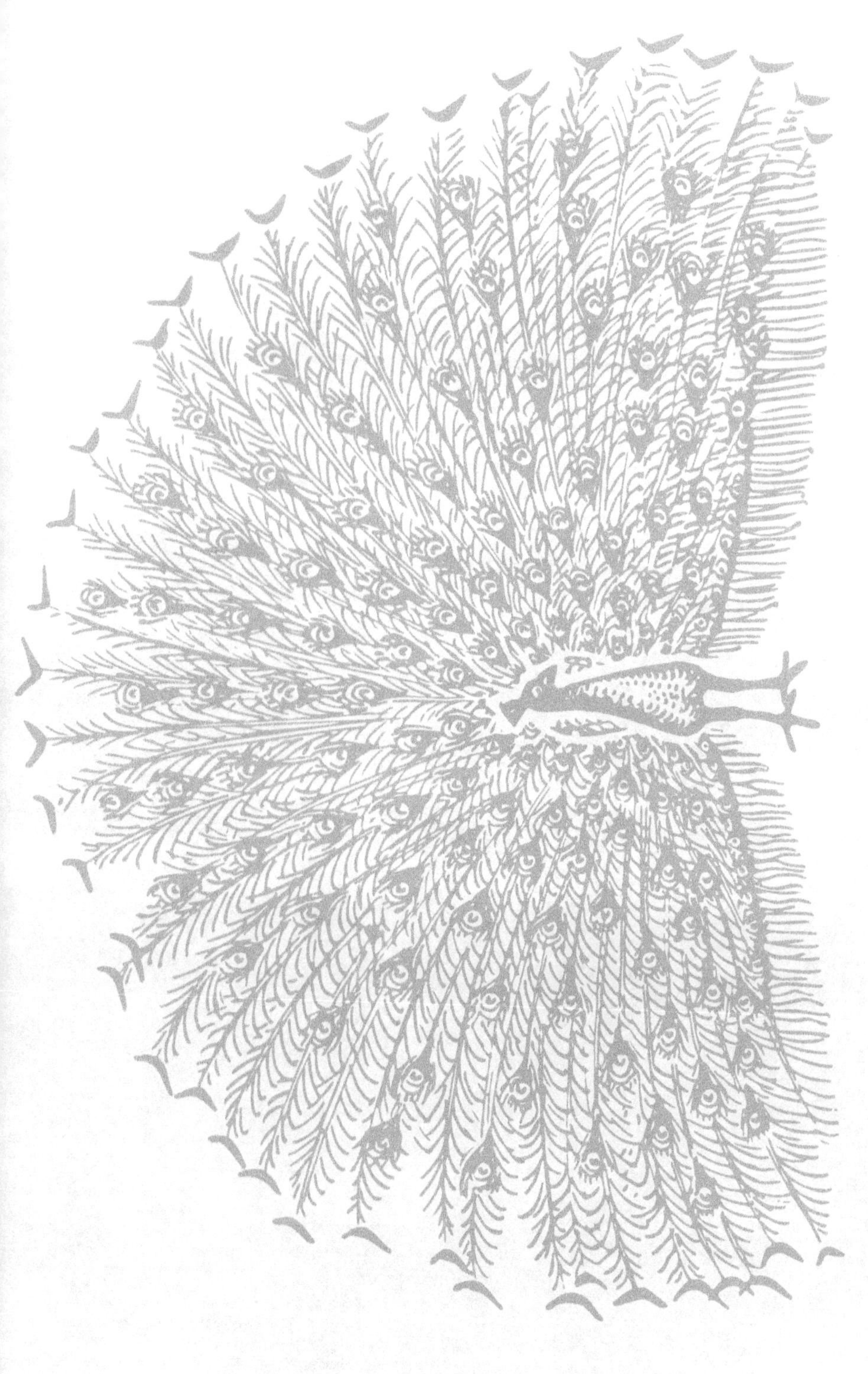

THANK YOU.

BIRDER!